IP Subnetting Quick Guide:

MASTER IN JUST 4 SIMPLE STEP IP
SUBNETTING OF ANY NETWORK

Table of content

Introduction

First of all, I want to thank you for reaching this point in the #LearnNetworking - IPv4 Concepts and Subnetting guide and thank you for making the decision to invest in yourself and to become better.

From this guide you can expect to get a better understanding of how the Internet works, how it grows and what are the trends in technology in the future with the rapid expansion of an Internet of Things (IoT)

At the end of each chapter you can expect practical exercises (subnetting or PC implementation of the elements studied). Each concept studied here can be applied to all existing devices on the market, be it IPv4 or IPv6.

PS: in case you have questions you can contact me via **email**, or on my **website.**

1) What is IP ?

The **IPv4 (or IP** – aka Internet Protocol) **protocol** was developed in the 1980s and it was designed to use **32 bits** of data in order to define an IP address (ex: **192.168.1.1**). As you can see in the example 192.168.1.1, there are 4 fields separated by dots and each field of these 4 can be allocated 8 bits of data:

8 bits * **4** fields = **32** bits.

Now let's think a bit about this number of bits, 32. It can tell us something about the maximum number of IP addresses that can be generated: $2 \wedge 32 \sim= $ **4.3 Billion**! Yeah, you read it well, 4.3 billion IPv4 addresses ... and the are **all allocated**.

TIP: why $2 \wedge 32$? because each bit can be 0 or 1, so if we have 32 bits we can generate about 4.3 billion unique numbers/addresses.

In 2011, exactly in the summer of that year, **IANA** (Internet Assigned Numbers Authority) has allocated the last IPv4 address space. Does that mean we can't connect other devices to the Internet anymore? Not at all. Since then, the Internet has grown a lot.

Here's a graph (figure 1.1) which predicts the growth of the Internet in terms of the connected devices:

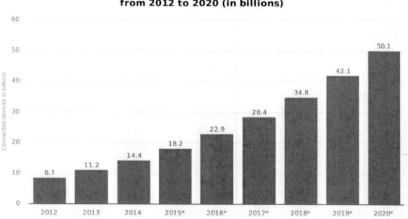

Figure 1.1

NOTE: please note that there is a difference between being allocated and being used. IANA has provided all of it's available IP addresses to the Service Providers (ISP) from around the world, but these addresses are far from being USED by the ISP (or more exactly used by us, the consumers)

As I said earlier, the maximum number of IPv4 addresses is ~**4.3 Billion**.

In 2016, it was estimated that the **total number** of **devices connected** to the **Internet** is around ~**20 billion**, which by far exceeds the IPv4 address number.

Due to this problem, measures have been taken to **slow IPv4 addressing** allocation by using techniques such as NAT (and also to introduce the concept of *Public and Private IP*). To another extent, far better than NAT is the introduction of the **IPv6 protocol**, which we will discuss a little bit later.

IPv4 Classes

As I said at the beginning of this chapter, each field (4 in total) of an IP address can have any value between **0 - 255** (8 bits / field, so 256 values,

$2 \wedge 8 = 256$). Thus, IP addresses are divided into several classes:

IP Class	Start IP	End IP	Network Prefix
A	1.0.0.0	127.255.255.255	1 - 127
B	128.0.0.0	191.255.255.255	128 - 191
C	192.0.0.0	223.255.255.255	192 - 223
D	224.0.0.0	239.255.255.255	224 - 239
E	240.0.0.0	255.255.255.255	240 - 255

Classes A, B and C are the ones **used in the Internet**, Class D being reserved for Multicast addresses and Class E is an experimental class that is not being used.

Public IP vs Private IP

Public IP addresses, as their name says, are used to communicate (transit) over the (Public) Internet and the **Private IP** addresses are used in Local Area Networks (**LANs**), such as our home's network or our school's network.

Thus, **Private IP addresses will never reach the Internet**. In order for us to be able to communicate over the Internet, a protocol such as **NAT** (Network Address Translation) was created with the purpose of *transforming Private IPs into Public IPs*.

Private IP Addresses

In the table below are the ranges of the Private IP addresses out there:

IP Class	Start IP	IP End	Network Prefix
A	10.0.0.1	10.255.255.255	10.0.0.0/8
B	172.16.0.1	172.31.255.255	172.16.0.0/12
C	192.168.0.1	192.168.255.255	192.168.0.0/16

NOTE: The rest of the IP addresses not mentioned in this table are PUBLIC !

Thus, we can have a scenario similar to the one in figure 1.2 below (multiple LANs - Network A and S - which contain private IP addressing and public IP addressing for the rest of the networks).

Also, these Private IP addresses (with the help of NAT) improves our **network's security** making it harder for potential attackers to enter it.

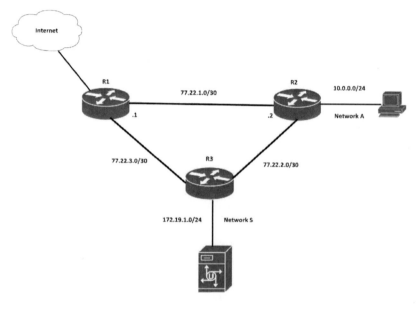

Figure 1.2

2) The Structure of an IPv4 Packet

In figure 1.3 you can see the structure (header) of an IPv4 packet

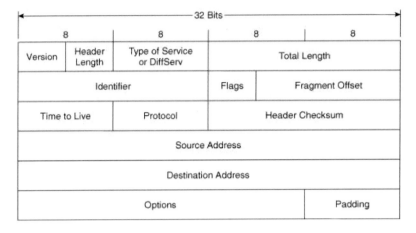

Figure 1.3

Here we can identify some important components that we'll interact with in many situations throughout our career:

- **IP Source Address**

- **IP Destination Address**

- **TTL** (Time to Live)

- **ToS** (Type of Service)

- **Header Checksum**

Now let's talk about each of these in more detail and we'll start with the IP addresses. I assume that it's clear the fact that in any communication between 2 devices we need a source address and a destination address.

In this case, the two fields (Source & Destination Address) are reserved for the **source IP** address and **destination IP** address.

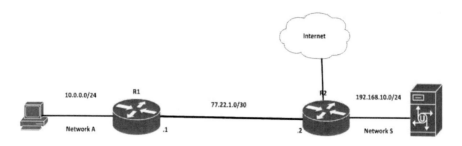

Figure 1.4

For example, in Figure 1.4 you can see the 2 networks: A and S. If the PC from Network A (with the IP 10.0.0.5) wants to communicate with the server (with the IP 192.168.10.8) from network S, then the source address of each packet will be **10.0.0.5** (PC's IP), and the destination address will be **192.168.10.8** (Server's IP).

Network loop prevention with TTL

Moving forward, there is another very important element within the IP header, known as **TTL** (Time to Leave). This element is a protection mechanism against **network loops** that might happen in the Internet (or in connections between Routers).

By default, the **value of TTL is 255** for each packet (but it can have a value between 1 - 255). This value **decreases** (on every hop) each time it **reaches another Router** (or another network). So, if we were to take the figure 1.3, when the PC sends a packet to the S server, the packets:

- Reach **R1** with a value of **255**

- Then R1 sends it to **R2** and the value will be updated to **254**

- In the end, the packets will reach the **S server** with a value of **253**

If there had been a misconfiguration on R2 and it would have thought that the server was directly connected to R1, then a **network loop would have been created** for R2 because it would have sent the packets back to R1 and R1 to would send them back to R2 (believing that the server is on R2's side).

This process would **go on and on** until the CPUs of the Routers would reach 100% workload, thus slowing the network down and at some point even causing downtime **infinitely** if the TTL had not existed.

If the **TTL value is equal to 0**, the Router which receives the packet will **drop it**.

In Figure 1.4 you can see multiple TTL values coming from multiple Internet sources (Yahoo, Google, CoreNetworkz). As you can see, the easiest way to find out the TTL is by using the **ping** command.

```
Command Prompt

C:\Users\sijugk>ping yahoo.com

Pinging yahoo.com [98.139.183.24] with 32 bytes of data:
Reply from 98.139.183.24: bytes=32 time=370ms TTL=39
Reply from 98.139.183.24: bytes=32 time=486ms TTL=39
Reply from 98.139.183.24: bytes=32 time=392ms TTL=38
Reply from 98.139.183.24: bytes=32 time=698ms TTL=38

Ping statistics for 98.139.183.24:
    Packets: Sent = 4, Received = 4, Lost = 0 (0% loss),
Approximate round trip times in milli-seconds:
    Minimum = 370ms, Maximum = 698ms, Average = 486ms

C:\Users\sijugk>ping Google.com

Pinging google.com [74.125.236.165] with 32 bytes of data:
Reply from 74.125.236.165: bytes=32 time=85ms TTL=52
Reply from 74.125.236.165: bytes=32 time=80ms TTL=52
Reply from 74.125.236.165: bytes=32 time=95ms TTL=52
Reply from 74.125.236.165: bytes=32 time=90ms TTL=52

Ping statistics for 74.125.236.165:
    Packets: Sent = 4, Received = 4, Lost = 0 (0% loss),
Approximate round trip times in milli-seconds:
    Minimum = 80ms, Maximum = 95ms, Average = 87ms

C:\Users\sijugk>ping corenetworkz.com

Pinging corenetworkz.com [192.64.119.167] with 32 bytes of data:
Reply from 192.64.119.167: bytes=32 time=384ms TTL=43
Reply from 192.64.119.167: bytes=32 time=420ms TTL=43
Reply from 192.64.119.167: bytes=32 time=376ms TTL=43
Reply from 192.64.119.167: bytes=32 time=371ms TTL=43
```

Figure 1.4

Version, ToS and Header Checksum

a. Version

The IP protocol can come in 2 different version:

1. IP version 4

2. IP version 6

Here, we're going to focus on IP version 4.

b. ToS (Type of Service)

ToS is an important element of QoS (Quality of Service). Basically, this field marks if a package needs to be treated in a special way (priority / VIP access: D)

In what situations does such a feature help us? In situations where we have **voice or video traffic** over the network (eg Skype calls - generally Skype for Business, WebEx).

QoS (or ToS) guarantees the quality of our services in real-time applications.

c) Header Checksum

The **checksum** of a packet helps with **maintaining** it's **integrity**. When we want to send traffic over the Internet, changes can take place along the way (packets can be lost, information can be altered, hackers can change the content). So we need a mechanism to ensure that it remains intact (aka. the **packet arrived** at the destination is **exactly the same** as the **one sent** from the source).

The checksum helps us achieve this goal. Basically it's a mathematical formula that generates a unique ID for every packet introduced into the formula. Thus, when Source (PC A) wants to send packets to Destination (Server S), each is passed through this formula, and their value is added to the "Header Checksum" field in IPv4.

When these packages arrive at the destination, it recalculates these IDs for each packet individually. If the **two values** (or IDs) - sent / received - are the same **then** the packets are the same (aka the **integrity** of the packets have been **retained** its integrity).

Other elements of the IP header

Here are the other elements that are included in the IP header:

- **Total Length** - of the header (in bytes)

- **Flags / Fragments Offset** - specifies if fragmentation is required for the packet

- **Options** - additional options for the IP packet (rarely used)

- **Protocol** - specifies the upper protocol being used (TCP or UDP)

- **Identifier** - unique identifier of the IP packet

- **Padding** - used to "adjust" the length of the packet in order for it to be a multiple of 32 (bits)

3) IP Subnetting

I P **subnetting** it's a very important aspect of the design and functionality (at optimal parameters) of computer networks. If it's not thought in an organized and efficient way it can lead to *increased costs* and *lower performance* of the network.

An **IPv4 address is made up of 32 bits**. Thus, it contains **4** fields (separated by dots) of **8 bits** each. Each of these fields can have a value between **0 - 255** (256 total values because, with the 8 bits, we can do: 2^8 = 256). Bellow you can see an example of a typical IP network:

192.168.0.0/24

192.168.0.0 = **network address** (think of it as the name of a *street*)

/24 = **network mask** (think of it as the maxim number of houses within a street)

Network Mask = indicates the size of a network (the **total number of IP addresses** that make up the network)

Now, let's take a in depth look of how an **IP address** looks like:

1. **The Network portion** - it's *size*, in bits, being dictated by the *network mask*

2. **The Host portion** - the remaining bits out of the total 32 (*32 bits - the network mask*)

Here is an example with the IP address, 192.168.0.0/24 which is a network address (similar to the name of a street)

/24 - represents the mask, meaning that the **first 24 bits** represent the **network portion**, and the remaining **8 bits** represents the **host portion.**

So if we want to allocate IP addresses on the 192.168.0.0 network then **the first 3 fields** will remain the **same (192.168.0)** and the last field will be used to **identify** *each device* (**from .1 to .254**). You can see an example on figure 1.5 of a computer network:

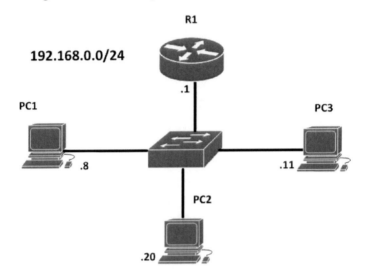

Figure 1.5

Example: 3 devices to which were are going to assign IP address from the network: 192.168.0.0/24

- 1st device: *192.168.0.8*

- 2nd device: *192.168.0.11*

- 3rd device: *192.168.0.20*

Beside this, the **Router** (aka. Default gateway) usually has the **first** (192.168.0.1) or the **last** (192.168.0.254) IP address in the network.

So the IP of R1 will be: 192.168.0.1

IP subnetting

IP subnetting is a technique used by network admins or designers which allows one to allocate a certain number of IP addresses for certain networks in order to accomplish a specific goal. Before we start with IP subnetting, we must first answer the following questions

1) **How many IP addresses can we generate with a given mask ? (ex: /24)**

2) **What's the 1st and the last IP address ?**

3) **Which IP addresses, from the network, can be used ?**

Example #1

Let's take the **192.168.0.0/24** network and answer the 3 questions:

1) 32 - 24 = 8, 2^8 = **256** - *max number* of IP addresses from a network mask of /24

2) **First IP**: 192.168.0.1, **Last IP**: 192.168.0.255 (Broadcast)

3) All of the following IP addresses *192.168.0.1 - 192.168.0.254* are usable in the network

Thus, the 192.168.0.0/24 network contains the following IP addresses:

192.168.0.1, 192.168.0.2, 192.168.0.3 ... 192.168.0.255

But, the **last** IP addresses (**192.168.0.255**) can't be used because it's the broadcast address (the address that's being used to reach all the devices within the network).

NOTE: only **254 IP addresses will be available** from the 256, because **the first address** (192.168.0.0 - network address) and **the last address** (192.168.0.255 - broadcast) **can not be used.** The reason being the fact that these addresses have a clear purpose: 1) to identify the network and 2) to send traffic to all devices in the network.

Example #2

Let's take another example with the **10.222.24.0/24** network and answer the 3 questions:

1) 32 - 24 = 8, 2^8 = 256 - max number of IP addresses from a network

mask of /24

2) **First IP:** 10.222.24.1, **Last IP**: 10.222.24.255 (Broadcast)

3) All of the following IP addresses *10.222.24.1 - 10.222.24.254* are usable in the network

Example #3

In this 3rd example, let's take the **172.22.9.0/27** network and answer the 3 questions:

1) 32 - 27 = 5, 2^5 = 32 - max number of IP addresses from a network mask of /27

2) **First IP:** 172.22.9.1, **Last IP**: 172.22.9.31

3) All of the following IP addresses *172.22.9.1 - 172.22.9.30* are usable in the network

Example #4

And the last example for this section will be with the **192.168.11.0/30** network:

1) 32 - 30 = 2, 2^2 = 4 - max number of IP addresses from a network mask of /30

2) **First IP:** 192.168.11.1, **Last IP**: 192.168.11.3

3) All of the following IP addresses 192.168.11.**1** - 192.168.11.**2** are usable in the network

So far, so good. Please do these exercises on paper to better understand the concept of subnetting (this is just the beginning: D).

"What's the next network ?"

In most of my courses, when I'm teaching subnetting, I ask this question: "So, guys, which is the next network?". And then lies a deep silence in the room. Nobody knows what to say (or more precisely what I mean) so let's see what's all about:

When it comes to subnetting, we are not only interested in the current network but also we are interested in the next network (after the current one). If we have the following network:

192.168.0.0/27

32 - 27 = 5, 2^5 = 32, in this scenario, **32,** represents the **total number of IP addresses** from a network with a mask of /27, but at the same time it *shows us the "delimitation"* between networks (or **32 is the increment**, as I like to say)

So, based on this principle **the next network** will be:

192.168.0.32/27, and then:

192.168.0.64/27

192.168.0.96/27

192.168.0.128/27

So, in increments of 32 for a network mask of /27. Take a look at the following table to see some other examples:

Network - IP	First IP	Last IP	Next Network
192.168.0.0/24	192.168.0.1	192.168.0.255	192.168.1.0/24
10.0.0.0/27	10.0.0.1	10.0.0.31	10.0.0.32/27
10.10.0.128/26	10.10.0.129	10.10.0.191	10.10.0.192/26

If we have a mask of **/24**, the *total number of IP addresses is 256.* For any field in an IP the **maximum value** can be between **0 - 255** (we can not have the number 256). We **can't** have this IP 192.168.0.256, but we can have 192.168.1.0. This example is similar to the following:

Let's make a visualization exercise and think of a watch. Think of the hour on this watch as being 11:59 (aka 192.168.0.255). In 1 minute we may have 11:60 ? No, of course not, but we can have 12:00 (aka 192.168.1.0). Well, the exact scenario happens in this situation:

Whenever we have a **network that ends** in (192.168.0) **.255** and we want to move on to the next network we'll have the value (192.168) **.1.0**

IP Subnetting based on the Number of Devices

Let's assume that after reading this book you received an offer to design the network of a firm. This business has 3 departments: *Sales, Marketing and IT.*

Each of these departments will have certain devices (Laptops, Printers, Servers, etc.) that **require an IP address to communicate** with each other and the Internet.

Suppose we need **15 IP** addresses for **Sales, 7** for **Marketing, 129** for **IT** and the **available address space** is the following: **10.23.0.0/16**

This addressing space will contain the following:

1) **/16** => 32 - 16 = 16, 2^16 = **65536** IP addresses

2) First IP: **10.23.0.1**, Last IP: **10.23.255.255** (Broadcast)

3) All of the following IP addresses **10.23.0.1 - 10.23.255.254** are usable within the network.

Think of each IP address as costing *$1 /month*. Our goal (with subnetting) is use **as few IP addresses** as **possible**, in order to reduce our costs. If we don't think/do it this way, we risk paying *$65,536 / month* only for the IPs!

Thus, we'll always start subnetting with the **biggest network** (based on the **total number** of IP addresses/devices **required**):

   1) 129 - IT

2) **15 - Sales**

3) **7 - Marketing**

Now, let's answer these questions:

1) What's the **netmask** ? - ex: /24

2) What's the **IP** address of the **network** ?

3) How many **IP** addresses are usable ?

4) What's the **IP** address of the **next network** ?

In order to find the **netmask** for each network we must first ask ourselves: "**which is the closest power of 2, greater than the number of devices ?**"

2^8	2^7	2^6	2^5	2^4	2^3	2^2	2^1	2^0
256	128	64	32	16	8	4	2	1

For example in case of the IT department, for **129** (the number of devices in the network) the closest power of 2 will be 8: **2^8 = 256.**

As I said before, **256** represents the **maximum number** of **IP** addresses, but we can't use all of them. *The reason being*: the **first** (.0) **address** is *reserved for the network*, and the **last** (.255) address is *reserved for Broadcast*.

So **we have to drop 2 IP addresses** out of the total 256. Thus, the result will be 256 - 2 = **254.** 254 will represent the total number of **usable IP addresses**.

Now we'll answer the above questions and also find the netmask number. First, we'll take the number (8) from the power of 2 and do:

1) **32 - 8 = 24** => **/24** represents the netmask

2) The network will be **10.23.0.0/24** (the difference between this network and the other one is the network mask - this one, with the /24, is much

smaller)

3) The following IP addresses: **10.23.0.1 - 10.23.0.254**, are included in the network

4) The **next network**: **10.23.1.0/24** (out of which we'll continue subnetting)

So, the 1st network is: **10.23.0.0/24**

In case of the *Sales* department, $2^5 = 32$ (actually is 32 - 2 = 30) is the closest value to **15** (the number of **required IP** addresses). We'll also take the power of 2 (which is 5) in order to find the netmask and also answer the other questions:

1) **32 - 5 = 27** => **/27** represents the netmask

2) The network is **10.23.1.0/27**

3) The following IP addresses: **10.23.1.1 - 10.23.1.30**, are included in the network

4) The **next network**: **10.23.1.32/27** (out of which we'll continue subnetting)

The 2nd network is: **10.23.1.0/27**

In case of the *Marketing* department, $2^4 = 16$ (actually is 16 - 2 = 14) is the closest value to 7 (the number of **required IP** addresses):

And here are the answers for the 4 questions:

1) **32 - 4 = 28** => **/28** represents the netmask

2) The network is **10.23.1.32/28**

3) The following IP addresses: **10.23.1.33 - 10.23.1.46** are included in the network

4) The **next network**: **10.23.1.48/28**

So, the 3rd network is: **10.23.1.32/28**

Exercise #1 Subnetting

Now is the time to put into practice what we've discussed until now. I'll invite you to complete the table below:

Network	First Address	Last Address	Broadcast Address	Next Network
173.22.50.0/24				
13.212.2.128/25				
13.22.1.0/27				
13.22.1.192/29				
92.68.2.64/26				
92.68.2.224/30				
84.88.32.24/29				
84.88.32.34/29				
44.55.66.77/26				
66.55.44.33/28				
11.22.33.44/30				
22.22.22.22/32				
44.11.22.59/25				

Exercise #2 Subnetting

In this 2nd exercise you will subnet a network according to the required IP addresses. Do not forget to **order the networks** in descending order (so you will start from the network with the highest number of required IP addresses).

Minimum IP Requirement	Network	Prima Adresa	Last Address	Broadcast Address	Next Network
Using the Address Space 172.22.96.0/19 allocate as efficiently as possible IP addresses for the following networks					
234 IP addresses					
32 IP addresses					
54 IP addresses					
278 IP addresses					
124 IP addresses					
2 IP addresses					
3 IP addresses					
10 IP addresses					
71 IP addresses					
150 IP addresses					
24 IP addresses					
39 IP addresses					
155 IP addresses					

After completing the exercise, as a BONUS we'll move forward and see how we can set up an IP address on Windows and on a Cisco Router.

4) Configuring an IP address on Windows 7/8/10

Let's take the example from the topology in figure 1.6 and configure an IP address on the PC and on the Cisco Router:

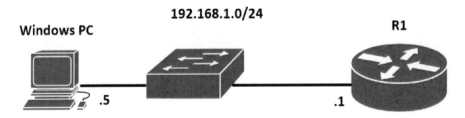

192.168.1.0/24

Windows PC   **R1**

.5   .1

Figure 1.6

On Windows, when it comes to setting up an IP address, we have 2 options (from the command line or from the GUI). First we'll start by checking our IP address from the command line:

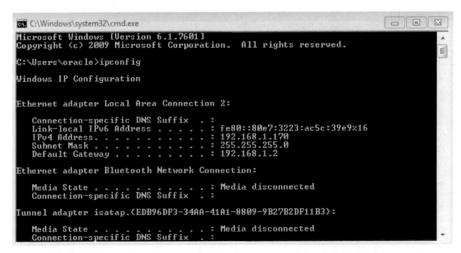

```
C:\Windows\system32\cmd.exe

Microsoft Windows [Version 6.1.7601]
Copyright (c) 2009 Microsoft Corporation.  All rights reserved.

C:\Users\oracle>ipconfig

Windows IP Configuration

Ethernet adapter Local Area Connection 2:

   Connection-specific DNS Suffix  . :
   Link-local IPv6 Address . . . . . : fe80::80e7:3223:ac5c:39e9%16
   IPv4 Address. . . . . . . . . . . : 192.168.1.170
   Subnet Mask . . . . . . . . . . . : 255.255.255.0
   Default Gateway . . . . . . . . . : 192.168.1.2

Ethernet adapter Bluetooth Network Connection:

   Media State . . . . . . . . . . . : Media disconnected
   Connection-specific DNS Suffix  . :

Tunnel adapter isatap.{EDB96DF3-34AA-41A1-8809-9B27B2DF11B3}:

   Media State . . . . . . . . . . . : Media disconnected
   Connection-specific DNS Suffix  . :
```

Figure 1.7

The command that's used in figure 1.7 is >**ipconfig** and as you can see, it shows us more information about the Ethernet (LAN), Wi-Fi, Bluetooth adapters. The most important elements shown by the command's output are:

- *IPv4 Address*

- *Network Mask*

- *Default gateway*

- *IPv6 Address*

All of these elements can be configured in one of 2 ways:

- **Statically** - we'll assign all of the info manually

- **Dynamically** - a protocol (such as DHCP) was configured on a server and assign dynamically

IP addresses with no human interaction at all.

Ok, now let's see how can we configure in Windows 7 (8.1 or 10) all of the elements mentioned above. In figures 1.8 and 1.9, you'll be able to see how can we do this:

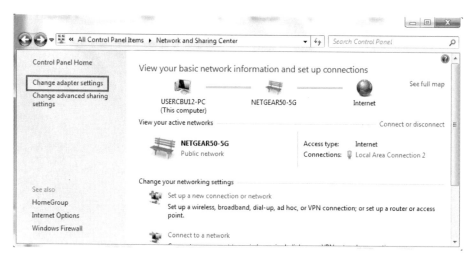

Figure 1.8

A very simple way to configure a **static IP address** is to go to the **"Control Panel -> Network and Sharing Center"** first, followed by **"Change adapter settings"** (or **Network and Internet -> Network**

Connections). Now you'll reach a window similar to the one shown in the figure below.

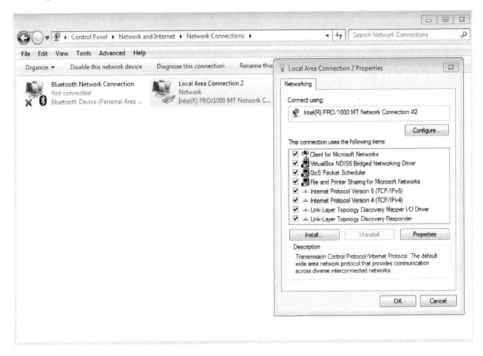

Figure 1.9

Here, we are looking for the "**Local Area Connection 2**" (in your case might be a similar name), and **right click** on it, followed by **"Properties"**. A new window will open, from which we'll **select IPv4** and then **click on Properties**. At this point we have reached a similar windows to the one in figure 1.10. Here we can (finally) set *the IP address, the Subnet Mask, Default Gateway and the DNS Server*:

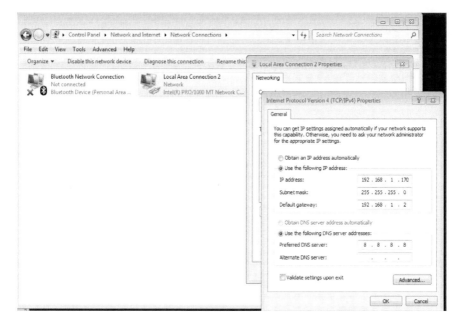

Figure 1.10

Now let's choose, for the sake of the example, a network from which we'll select the other elements required to have access to the Internet. The network's IP address will be 192.168.1.0/24, out of which **192.168.1.170** will be assigned to the PC (Windows 7). The **/24** in decimal mask looks 255.255.255.0 and the **default gateway** (the Internet-connected Router) will have the IP address of 192.168.1.2.

We also need to set the **DNS** server (the one that helps us with the name resolution: from a domain (ex: google.com) will provide us with its IP address (ex: 216.58.214.227)) with the IP address of **8.8.8.8**

Now that we're done with all of these settings, we can check our configuration (from CMD) using the following commands:

>**ping 8.8.8.8**   //checks the Internet connection(actually to 8.8.8.8, which

is Google's server)

>**ping google.ro**   //checks the DNS service **and** the Internet connection

>**nslookup google.ro**   //checks the DNS service

23

5) Configuring an IP address on the Router

Now, let's configure an IP addresses on a Cisco Router (R1 from figure 1.6). So, a Router **interconnects** multiple networks through **ports** (usually 2 or 3). We are calling **port** a physical place where a cable can be plugged. The other name that we assign to the logical part of a port is **interface**.

So, to sum things up:

- **Port = Physical**

- **Interface = Logical**

For example: *"we will set an **IP** (logical) address on an **interface** and connect the cable (physically) to a **port"***

These interfaces must have an IP address configured to communicate within the network and the interface must be turned **ON**. In figure 1.11, you can see how we can set an IP address on an interface:

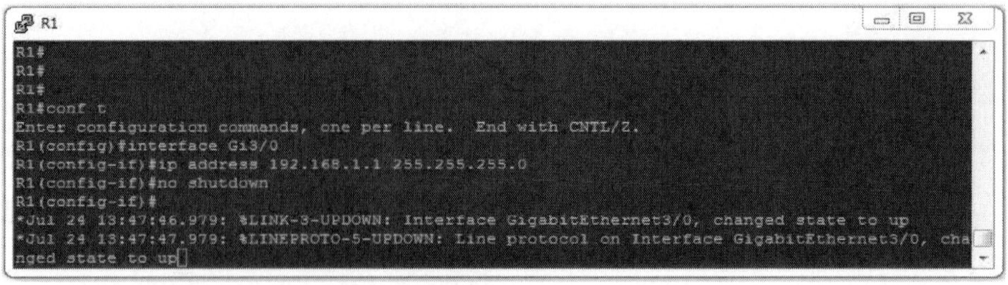

Figure 1.11

R1(config)#**interface** FastEthernet0/0

R1(config-if)#**ip address** 192.168.1.1 255.255.255.0

R1(config-if)#**no shutdown**

And that's it ! Now we have a fully working network and we have the ability to further connect to the Internet or communicate with other devices in our local networks.

Enjoyed the book? Please leave a Review on Amazon.com

If you received value from this book, then I'd like to ask you for a favour. Would you be kind enough to leave a review for this book on Amazon.

Click here here to leave a Review on Amazon.com

I would like to thank you for reading this book and reaching to the end of it (trust me when I say, that not many people manage to get this far away).

Also, I want to reach as many people as I can with this book (my goal is 10.000 people in the next 3 years). That's a lot of people and without you and your review I won't be able to achieve that.

Not only that, but you will receive some good karma that sooner or later will manifest into your life.

Thank you!

Ramon Nastase

Made in United States
North Haven, CT
04 February 2022

15699218R00017